Lessons in
LEADERSHIP
from the
GREATEST
GENERATION

Lessons in
LEADERSHIP
from the
GREATEST
GENERATION

ROD GRAGG

PELICAN PUBLISHING COMPANY
Gretna 2013

The word "Pelican" and the depiction of a pelican are
trademarks of Pelican Publishing Company, Inc., and are
registered in the U.S. Patent and Trademark Office.

Library of Congress Cataloging-in-Publication Data

Gragg, Rod.
  Lessons in leadership from the greatest generation / Rod Gragg.
    pages cm
  ISBN 1-4556-1821-7 (hardcover : alk. paper) — ISBN 978-1-4556-1822-4
(e-book) 1. Leadership. I. Title.
  HD57.7.G7293 2013
  658.4'092—dc23

                                    2013019075

Printed in the United States of America
Published by Pelican Publishing Company, Inc.
1000 Burmaster Street, Gretna, Louisiana 70053

In memory of two leaders from the Greatest Generation:

Sgt. Lemuel Wallace "Skip" Gragg
U.S. 725th Military Police Battalion
and
Sgt. William N. "Bill" Outlaw, Jr.
42nd Bombardment Group, U.S. 13th Air Force

Greater love hath no man than this,
that a man lay down his life for his friends.

John 15:13

Contents

Preface

I was raised in the company of heroes.

As a "Baby Boomer" growing up in the 1950s and '60s, I saw them everywhere: at church, at school, at movies, at restaurants, at stores. They were there at sporting events, family reunions, the neighbor's house. They were my friends' fathers, my doctors, my bosses, my uncles, my dad.

They were the veterans of World War II—and to me, they were all heroes. No Americans of any era faced greater challenges, shouldered greater responsibilities, or were willing to take greater risks, all for what was right. No matter whether they were the few who saw combat or the many who supported front-line troops, they were heroes to me. And so were the people who loved them and waited for their return. Long before I ever heard the phrase "the Greatest Generation," I thought they were. Even as a boy, I knew that I was blessed to be living in the company of heroes.

I watched them. I listened. And I learned. Later, as a professional historian working on World War II books, documentaries, and oral-history projects, I interviewed scores of them. Knowing them, hearing their stories, and learning of their lives and values became one of the most meaningful blessings of my life. Over time, as the Greatest Generation began passing into history, I realized that their extraordinary achievements came from the core values taught them by their nineteenth-century parents. And I also came to understand that, regardless of their personal faith, those values made so many of them natural leaders.

Sadly, as the Greatest Generation now leaves us, the core values they learned as children—the values on which our nation was founded and flourished—appear to be steadily diminishing in our culture. And America needs them now more than ever. Here, in this small book, is a lasting legacy from the American men and women who weathered the Great Depression and won the greatest war in history—ten vitally important lessons in leadership from the Greatest Generation. They'll still work today, if we faithfully follow them.

Acknowledgments

The camera was off and the microphone had been removed when I asked a World War II veteran an off-the-cuff question. He was a combat veteran from the Pacific Theater of Operations, an army paratrooper who had been engaged in close-up, sometimes hand-to-hand combat on an almost daily basis for more than ninety consecutive days. After conducting oral-history interviews with World War II veterans for almost a decade, I had heard a lot of unforgettable stories, but none more riveting than his. "What do people say when you tell them this story?" I asked. His answer: "I don't know—you're the first person I've ever told it to." When I asked why, he replied, "You're the first person who ever asked me about it." That extraordinary modesty is one of the principal character traits that distinguishes the Greatest Generation. It's a key ingredient of the "lead-by-example" attitude that is so common among that generation. Writing this book was a powerful reminder that I have been blessed to have spent so much time in the company of such remarkable Americans. As I acknowledge the people who helped me produce this important little volume, I must first say to the many World War II veterans I have known—and to their spouses and families—*thank you* for the way you have so enriched my life and the extraordinary lessons you have taught me.

A sincere thank-you is due to my dear friend and mentor, Harry Reeder, pastor of Briarwood Presbyterian Church in Birmingham, Alabama, whose work on leadership—*The Leadership Dynamic*— introduced me to the Bible-based principles of leadership that inspired the Greatest Generation and this book. I'm also grateful to the administration of Coastal Carolina University and our board of advisors for their support of the Center for Military and Veterans Studies at CCU. Thanks also to Kathleen Calhoun Nettleton, the publisher and president of Pelican Publishing Company; Editor in Chief Nina Kooij; and Terry Callaway, Pelican's production director, for the remarkable talent and expertise they brought to this work. Many thanks too to my literary agent and friend, Joel Kneedler of Alive Communications. I'm very thankful as well to the late Mike Fitch, D-Day veteran and my friend, for his time, knowledge, and quietly inspirational example. Lifelong lessons in character and leadership were bestowed on me by two beloved members of the Greatest Generation: my father, L. W. "Skip" Gragg, and my father-in-law, William N. "Bill" Outlaw, Jr. They are sorely missed, but their wonderful legacy continues.

I'm also grateful to Bob Patrick, the director of the Veterans History Project at the Library of Congress, for the critically important work that he and his staff perform as they collect and preserve oral history from American veterans of all eras. My sincere thanks also to the staff of the General George Patton

Museum and Center of Leadership; the Dwight D. Eisenhower Presidential Library; the U.S. Army Military History Institute; the U.S. Army Military History Center; the National Museum of the U.S. Air Force; the National Museum of the U.S. Marine Corps; the National Museum of the U.S. Navy; the Airborne and Special Operations Museum; the Airborne Museum at Ste. Mère Eglise in Normandy; the Lincoln County Museum in North Platte, Nebraska; the National Archives; the U.S. Army Medical Department; the National Portrait Gallery; the Marine Corps Archive in Quantico, Virginia; the U.S. Navy Historical Foundation; the World War II Foundation; and the staff of the Prints and Photographs Division of the Library of Congress. I deeply appreciate the encouragement and kind words from my friends Pat Williams and Larkin Spivey.

Much appreciation is also due to: George Goldfinch; Mark Roach; Stovall Witte, Jr.; David Frost; Dr. Bob Squatriglia; Wilma Fitch; Dennis Reed; David Parker; the Reverend Randy Riddle; Mrs. William N. Outlaw; Delores Lunsford; Deborah Outlaw; Ted and Connie Gragg; Joe and Margaret Outlaw; Doug and Jackie Rutt; John and Tina Outlaw; Jimmy and Gail Outlaw; Newt Outlaw; Faith and Troy Roehm; Rachel and Jay Lindsey; Elizabeth and Jon Comer; Joni Gragg Hill; Penny and Ryan McCrackin; Skip Gragg; Matt Gragg; Miranda Whitaker — and Kylah, Sophia, Cody, Jaxon, Gracie, Ashlyn, and Jate. I'm very thankful to the loving legacy bequeathed to me by another extraordinary member of the Greatest Generation, my mother, Elizabeth Lunsford Gragg. Finally, a uniquely special and loving thank-you is due my wife and the love of my life — Cindy Outlaw Gragg. And I am eternally grateful for the reality of Isaiah 53:5.

Lessons in
LEADERSHIP
from the
GREATEST
GENERATION

Lesson in Leadership #1

Real Leaders
Have a Vision

★ ★ ★ ★

Young Chester Nimitz wanted to be a soldier.

Adm. Chester Nimitz.
(Library of Congress)

Thankfully, he couldn't get into West Point. Instead, he became a sailor in the U.S. Navy—and eventually a high-ranking admiral. And it was in the navy, as commander of the United States Pacific Fleet, that his extraordinary leadership skills and vision proved to be critical to the Allied victory in World War II.

The American Armed Forces faced an enormous challenge. The United States had to fight a two-front world war—against Imperial Japan on one side of the world and Nazi Germany on the other. Militarily, both enemies were more experienced and better prepared. On December 7, 1941, the Japanese surprise attack on Pearl Harbor simultaneously plunged America into the war and also destroyed much of the U.S. Navy's Pacific Fleet. The losses were staggering: More than 2,000 Americans were killed.

Almost 1,200 were wounded. Twenty-one warships were sunk or seriously damaged—including eight battleships. Almost half the American aircraft in Hawaii were destroyed.

Japan's military dictatorship believed that its surprise attack on Pearl Harbor would keep the United States out of the war, or at least neutralize America long enough for Imperial Japan to conquer the Pacific rim and much of Asia, putting millions of people under a brutal fascist dictatorship. But the Japanese planners underestimated the will and determination of the Greatest Generation.

America came back—quickly.

Little more than six months after Pearl Harbor, American forces had stopped and reversed the Japanese conquest. But it wasn't easy. In 1942, Japan's empire stretched more than four thousand miles across the Pacific Ocean from the waters off Australia to the Aleutian Islands of Alaska—roughly the same distance as between Miami, Florida and Juneau, Alaska. It was

As naval launches search for survivors, the sunken battleship USS Arizona *continues to burn above the waterline. Of the 2,402 Americans killed in the Japanese surprise attack on Pearl Harbor, 1,177 died aboard the* Arizona. (Library of Congress)

one of history's most remarkable comebacks. And it was due in no small part to Rear Adm. William Chester Nimitz, who—at almost sixty years of age—provided much of the leadership that won the war in the Pacific.

Nimitz commanded the U.S. Pacific Fleet, directed operations over a giant span of the Pacific, and coordinated with American ground forces under the command of Gen. Douglas MacArthur. Victory in the Pacific was a coordinated effort by the Army, Navy, and Marine Corps, and it required a critically important leadership attribute that Admiral Nimitz possessed in abundance—a vision for success.

Nimitz skillfully oversaw the rapid rebuilding of the naval fleet so severely damaged at Pearl Harbor. He unleashed American submarines on Japanese shipping, disrupting troops reinforcements and slashing fuel supplies. And he executed two brilliant strategies that eventually crippled Japan's military empire. First, he shifted the focus of American naval strategy from battleships to aircraft carriers. Through his visionary leadership, carrier-based American air power became the U.S. Navy's mighty fist in the Pacific. He demonstrated its power in May of 1942, when the U.S. Navy stopped the Japanese drive across the South Pacific with a key strategic victory at the battle of the Coral Sea. A few weeks later—at the battle of Midway—he ambushed the main Japanese fleet and decisively defeated it, sending four Japanese aircraft carriers to the bottom of the Pacific. And all of them had attacked Pearl Harbor.

It was the turning point of World War II in the Pacific: after Midway, Japanese forces would always be on the defensive. It would take three more years of bloody fighting to drive Japanese forces back to Japan and surrender—but that too would be greatly

A U.S. Navy "Dauntless" dive bomber, launched from the aircraft carrier USS Hornet, prepares to attack the Japanese fleet at the battle of Midway in June of 1942. The U.S. Navy dealt Imperial Japan a decisive blow at Midway, which halted Japanese expansion in the Pacific. (Library of Congress)

determined by another visionary strategy executed by Chester Nimitz. Japanese troops were embedded in force on countless islands across the Pacific, and the cost of defeating them could be horrible, as courageous American marines learned at the bloody battle of Tarawa. The Japanese dictatorship had taught its soldiers to be fanatical—to fight to the last man. Clearing every island on the way to Japan could have shredded American forces and prolonged the war for years, which is what the Japanese leadership counted on.

But Chester Nimitz had vision. He refused to fight the war on the enemy's terms. Instead, he skillfully executed an extraordinary strategy called "island-hopping." **He refused to** Rather than fighting every Japanese soldier on every Japanese-held **fight the war** island, only the key islands were attacked and captured. The others **on the enemy's** were bypassed. The Japanese **terms.** troops on them were left without food, supplies, or anyone to fight. They were isolated, left to "wither on the vine," as General MacArthur put it. As American forces under Nimitz and MacArthur steadily drove the Japanese invaders back to Japan, a parade of obscure islands became a roll-call of valor for the American Armed Forces: Tarawa, Guadalcanal, the Gilberts, the Solomons, the Marshalls, the Marianas, Truk, Saipan, Rabaul, Leyte, Mindanao, Iwo Jima, Okinawa, and others. At the battle of Leyte Gulf in October of 1944, Nimitz's naval forces decisively destroyed what remained of the Japanese Navy.

By island-hopping from one key base to another—not wasting lives, resources, or time—American forces steadily advanced across the Pacific, building airstrips on principal islands along the way and using them to bomb targets in Japan. And finally, the Japanese military dictatorship surrendered. Tens of thousands of American lives were saved—and perhaps hundreds of thousands of Japanese lives. When Imperial Japan's military commanders surrendered aboard the USS *Missouri* in Tokyo Bay, ending World War II, the Allied victory was due in great measure to the leadership of Adm. Chester Nimitz, who realized that real leaders have a vision: they understand the mission and they're committed to it.

Real Leaders Are Self-Starters

★ ★ ★ ★

In May of 1945, amid the horrors of combat, Cpl. James Day proved this lesson.

Cpl. James L. Day.
(reconmarine.com)

He was a young marine from East St. Louis who found himself at the bloodiest battle in the Pacific theater of World War II — the battle of Okinawa.

Imperial Japan's military dictatorship had trained Japanese troops to fight to the death, and on Okinawa, they did. One step from the Japanese homeland, the island was considered to be Japanese soil. Commanders told the Japanese troops defending it that if they surrendered, they would dishonor their families, their nation, and their emperor. And so they fought to the death. Of the 110,000 Japanese troops on Okinawa, approximately 90 percent were killed.

James Day was a squad-leader in the Sixth Marine Division, and at Okinawa his squad was sent out ahead of the marine front line as forward observers. Almost immediately, Corporal Day and his squad came under a barrage of Japanese mortar and artillery fire, and when it ended, they were attacked by a Japanese Banzai charge. Corporal Day directed a powerful return fire, which turned back the enemy assault—but half his squad was killed or wounded. Soon it was dark, and the Japanese made repeated attacks. Three times in quick succession, Japanese troops came screaming out of the night in Banzai charges. Corporal Day and his squad stopped them all—but more marines were killed and more were wounded. As the hours passed that night, Day could hear the wounded marines calling out in the darkness for corpsmen (medics).

But there were no medics.

Corporal Day listened to the heart-rending cries of his wounded buddies until he couldn't take it anymore. He decided someone

U.S. Marines on Okinawa engage the enemy. The battle lasted from April 1 to June 22, 1945, and claimed more lives than any engagement in the Pacific theater—12,513 Americans and more than 95,000 Japanese. (National Archives)

U.S. Marines move cautiously over battle-torn terrain on Okinawa. (U.S. Army Signal Corps)

had to do something—and *he* was that someone. So he crawled through the darkness until he found one of the wounded marines, hoisted him on his back, and raced back toward the main marine line. The Japanese

He decided someone *had* to do something— and *he* was that someone.

heard him and opened a searing fire, but he made it. He could have stayed there—in safety—but he didn't. Back he went and found another wounded man, carrying him to the rear under heavy fire. And then he did it again, and again. He carried four of his fellow marines to the rear under savage enemy fire—and saved their lives.

That was more than enough selfless courage for any man at any time, but Corporal Day went back to his forward position and manned a light machine gun, just in time for another Japanese Banzai charge. Only a handful of marines were still able to fight, but they turned back the attack—thanks mainly to Corporal Day and his machine gun at the point. This time, however, he was wounded. And his machine gun was destroyed. He lay there in the darkness, wounded, with no machine gun. Why not slip away in the night and seek safety? Who could have blamed him? But James Day knew if the Japanese got by him, other marines in his rear would have to fight them, so he chose to stay. He scrounged around in the darkness, gathered rifles from fallen marines—and waited.

The Japanese soon attacked again. Day led the few surviving marines in such a fierce defense—pouring fire into the charging enemy line—that the Japanese assault collapsed. The next day, the Japanese attacked again, but Day and his surviving squad members again stopped them—with the last attackers falling just feet from Day's foxhole. Finally, the fighting ended. Marine reinforcements reached Corporal Day's forward position, and he was taken to the rear for medical treatment. And then his fellow marines counted the enemy bodies lying in front of Corporal Day's foxhole.

They numbered more than one hundred.

It turned out that Corporal Day, and the handful of marines with him, had been battling a major Japanese assault—and near the end, Corporal Day had almost singlehandedly stopped a key part of it. For that, Cpl. James Day was awarded the Congressional Medal of Honor, at age nineteen. But to him, the greater honor was the headcount nobody could truly make: no one could really calculate how many American lives had been saved by his heroic actions.

Even though it meant risking everything, Cpl. James Day did not wait to be prodded into action. Because he understood a principal lesson of leadership: real leaders are self-starters.

Lesson in Leadership #3

Real Leaders Always Take Responsibility

★ ★ ★ ★

Generals didn't usually chat with privates.

Maj. Gen. Dwight D. Eisenhower. (National Archives)

But this one did.

At 10:00 P.M. English time on June 5, 1944, American paratroopers of the 101st and 82nd Airborne divisions were lined up beside their C-47 troop transports on airstrips in southern Britain, waiting for the order to board their aircraft. The Allied invasion of France was finally under way, and in a couple of hours, in the early-morning darkness of D-Day—June 6, 1944—they would parachute from their C-47s or land in gliders behind the German lines in Normandy. Just before they received the order to take to the skies, some of them got a visit from Maj. Gen. Dwight D. Eisenhower.

Eisenhower was the Supreme Allied Commander in Europe and the mastermind of "Operation Overlord"—the D-Day invasion of France. In just hours he would order more than 100,000 American and Allied military personnel into harm's way. It would be the mightiest amphibious attack in history, aimed at the coast of Normandy. If successful, it would break through Adolf Hitler's formidable coastline defenses — the infamous Atlantic Wall — and launch the Allied drive to free Europe from Nazi enslavement. In an official statement read to the young Americans preparing for battle, Eisenhower admitted that the challenge they faced was "not an easy one" but that freedom for millions of people depended upon them. "The eyes of the world are upon you," he reminded them. "The hopes and prayers of liberty loving people everywhere march with you."

Then, he went to see the first troops leave for battle, to talk in person with the soldiers of the American airborne divisions that would open the D-Day fighting. He walked among the ranks of

On the eve of D-Day, June 6, 1944, General Eisenhower — the Supreme Allied Commander in Europe — chats with paratroopers of the 101st Airborne. Soon afterward, these troops would be in the skies over France, and many would not return. (National Archives)

the 101st Airborne—the 502nd Parachute Infantry Regiment. He talked to the men, asking where they were from, chatting about fishing and baseball, speaking with them about the home they all loved and were willing to die for: *that* America.

He was trying to encourage *them* — but, typical of the Greatest Generation, *they* encouraged *him*.

"Quit worrying, General," one paratrooper told him. "We'll take care of this thing for you."

Eisenhower stood on the edge of the runway until midnight, watching his soldiers head for battle until the last aircraft disappeared in the darkness. Soon afterward, the young paratroopers reached the dark skies over Normandy—which were quickly illuminated by German anti-aircraft fire. The paratroopers had the job of setting up the invasion, seizing and holding key roadways, bridges, and crossroads for the main Allied force landing on the beaches. Some of them were shot out of the sky when enemy anti-aircraft fire hit their planes. Some parachuted to the earth, weighed down with equipment, and drowned in marshes and rivers. Others were killed when their gliders, skidding across fields the Germans had flooded, crashed into hedgerow fences. But most made it. And as ordered, they fought hard, captured their objectives—and held back German reinforcements until the main invasion force could move in from the beaches.

The Allied landings occurred soon after dawn as planned. Troops poured ashore, broke through the German defenses, and pushed inland from four of the five Allied beaches—from Utah, Gold, Juno, and Sword. But on one American beach, the D-Day invasion was slammed to a halt. The beach was code-named

Weighed down by his parachute, gear, and Thompson submachine gun, an American paratrooper boards his C-47 troop carrier for the D-Day airborne drop. (National Archives)

"Omaha" — and would forever be remembered as "Bloody Omaha."

There, the beachside bluffs were high. The defenses were strong. The German defenders were tough. The American aerial bombing and the naval bombardment had failed to destroy many of the German defenses. And the first wave of American troops ashore was decimated — men of the U.S. First and Twenty-Ninth Infantry divisions. A second wave landed. And it too was slaughtered in many places. More troops landed, and they too suffered severe casualties. At 8:30 A.M., the landings were stopped, and the troops were on their own. Hours passed with no breakthrough. The holdup at Bloody Omaha threatened the entire invasion.

It was no fault of General Eisenhower's. His planning and coordination had been brilliant. If D-Day failed, the blame surely would not fall on him. But if it had failed, Dwight D. Eisenhower was prepared to take full responsibility for it. Besides his closest aides, no one knew that the general had composed a secret message for use if necessary. It was a handwritten official statement that Eisenhower had drafted even before the invasion began, intended to be released to America and the world if the Allied landings on D-Day proved to be a failure.

In it, Eisenhower praised the Allied forces for "bravery and devotion to duty." They deserved no blame, he stated. Any lack of success was not *their* fault. The failure of D-Day, he wrote, would be *his* responsibility and his alone. The statement was never needed. D-Day did not fail. With the help of courageous U.S. Navy commanders, who took their destroyers perilously close to shore and blasted the enemy defenses at close range, the

Known only to his closest aides, General Eisenhower prepared this message to be released to the world if the D-Day landings failed. (National Archives)

American troops on **It would be *his*** Bloody Omaha finally fought their way off the **responsibility and** beach, drove back the **his alone.** German defenders, and headed inland. Allied forces advancing from the beachheads linked up with the paratroopers and began driving the Germans back across France.

D-Day was a tremendous success, and in less than one year, Nazi Germany was defeated and V-E Day — "Victory in Europe" — was being celebrated by Americans everywhere. As for General Eisenhower? Within a few years he would become *President* Eisenhower — due largely to his leadership as the Supreme Allied Commander.

Dwight D. Eisenhower, the man credited by history as the victor of D-Day, understood a central truth of leadership: real leaders always take responsibility.

Lesson in Leadership #4

Real Leaders
Persevere

You've probably never heard of Elaine Wright.

Eager servicemen hurry from their train into the USO canteen at North Platte, Nebraska. By war's end, the volunteers at the little canteen would have served more than six million Americans in uniform. (Lincoln County Historical Museum, North Platte, Nebraska)

She didn't wear a uniform or go to war. And she wasn't famous.

Even so, Elaine Wright was a real leader. During World War II, she was a volunteer at the USO canteen in North Platte, Nebraska. The USO was a private, nonprofit agency; the United Service Organizations was its official name. It was composed of a half-dozen groups: the Salvation Army, the YMCA, the YWCA, the National Jewish Welfare Board, the National Catholic Community Service, and the National Traveler's Aid Association. Its goal was to bring encouragement, comfort, recreation, and entertainment to American soldiers, sailors, and marines throughout the world. And to the men and women of the American Armed Forces in World War II, it was known simply as the USO.

38

It became famous for its Camp Shows, which presented performances by big-name entertainers and Hollywood stars at American military posts, camps, and bases at home and in combat zones. Actors and actresses such as Bob Hope, Marlene Dietrich, Gary Cooper, Lucille Ball, and Dinah Shore joined musical, dance, and comedy performers such as the Andrew Sisters, Lena Horne, Fred Astaire, Bing Crosby, and the Marx Brother to briefly brighten the lives of Americans. At home and around the world, the USO organized more than 400,000 performances for American military personnel during World War II. The Camp Shows made the newsreels and boosted military morale. But that wasn't what endeared the USO to most young Americans in uniform.

It was the USO canteen.

Set up in churches, storefronts, bus stops, and railway stations,

A volunteer serves punch to a soldier in a Washington, D.C. USO canteen. Wherever American soldiers, sailors, and marines served in World War II, the USO was there. (Library of Congress)

USO canteens reached out to soldiers, sailors, and marines near bases, posts, camps, and portside—and at travel sites where they stopped momentarily en route to some distant, dangerous wartime destination. The canteens offered Americans in uniform "a home away from home" with simple but priceless comforts: a hot cup of coffee, a cold glass of lemonade, a warm smile. USO canteens were hosted and operated by dedicated civilian volunteers—women mainly—and one of those volunteers was Elaine Wright.

She was a middle-aged wife and mom living in North Platte when World War II began. It was a small Midwestern town of 12,000 people perched alongside the North Platte River on the high plains of Nebraska. Pleasant, quiet, and postcard cheerful, it was perfect for growing corn, harvesting wheat, raising cattle, and producing patriots. But it was nowhere near an army post,

The volunteer staff at the North Platte Canteen included homemaker Elaine Wright, seated on the far left of the front row in this wartime image. (Lincoln County Historical Museum, North Platte, Nebraska)

navy yard, or marine base. However, the Union Pacific Railroad ran right through the middle of little North Platte, and within weeks of Pearl Harbor, railway cars packed with young Americans bound for war were rolling through. And there, on the prairie of Nebraska, the trains paused momentarily so the steam locomotives could take on water.

Elaine Wright and the other women of North Platte saw an opportunity. And they seized it. On Christmas Day of 1941, they set up a USO canteen at the North Platte railway station. It was stocked with hot coffee, fried chicken, homemade sandwiches, donuts, cookies, cake, cigarettes, magazines, and friendly faces. The women received no government support. Instead, they furnished the food, coffee, cigarettes, and magazines themselves, supplemented by cash donations made by local businesses, farmers, and schoolchildren. When funds ran low, they held dances, organized scrap-metal drives, and hosted movie benefits to raise money. It wasn't unusual for the North Platte Canteen to use 45 pounds of coffee in a single day — along with 100 pounds of meat, 175 loaves of bread, two quarts of peanut butter and 500 bottles of milk. Volunteers were known to hand out twenty home-baked birthday cakes in a single day.

Typically, a troop train paused in North Platte for only ten minutes — but canteen volunteers made the most of those precious moments. In the station waiting room, someone pounded out a cheerful tune on an old piano. Others passed out the coffee, sandwiches, cookies, milk, and magazines. One volunteer called out for anyone celebrating a birthday — and presented the surprised celebrant with a freshly baked cake to share with his buddies. Then they cheered the troops as they reboarded the train.

It all lasted only about ten minutes. Then the train was gone. And the station was empty of uniforms. But the USO volunteers had made a difference. Recalled an old soldier sixty years later, "They made us feel like we were heroes."

Elaine Wright was right there in the middle of it, making sandwiches, pouring coffee, handing out cookies, welcoming the troops along with all the other volunteers. She and her husband, who worked for the railroad, had one son, and he had joined the navy for the duration of the war. Once Elaine confided to another worker that she liked to imagine her son in some faraway place, being cheered and served by a USO volunteer.

One day she failed to show up at the canteen.

Nobody criticized her—she had done more than her share—but it wasn't like Elaine not to be there without some explanation. Someone made inquiries, and the other volunteers learned the terrible news. Elaine and her husband had received the War Department telegram that every family feared: their son had been killed in action. He was their only son. And now he would not come home—ever. If Elaine had never returned to the canteen, everyone would have understood. Every soldier, sailor, and marine whom she greeted would remind her of her lost son. It was only natural that she would stay home and grieve.

But she didn't.

A few days after she received the crushing news, Elaine Wright was back at the North Platte Canteen, making sandwiches, handing out cookies, pouring coffee. She had **And so she went on with her important work.**

chosen to persevere. "I can't help *my* son," she said, "but I can help *someone else's* son." And so she went on with her important work. By war's end, Elaine Wright and the other volunteers at the USO canteen in tiny North Platte, Nebraska had served more than six million Americans in uniform. For generations to come, their unselfish service would stand as a memorial to the contribution of American civilians in World War II. Why?

Because Elaine Wright, and others like her, understood a major maxim of leadership: real leaders don't give up easily—they persevere.

★ ★ ★ ★

Real Leaders Always Take Care of Their People

★ ★ ★ ★

Almost 2,700 Americans learned this lesson one afternoon in 1942, while they were prisoners of war.

Cdr. Richard N. Antrim.
(U.S. Navy Historical Foundation)

They learned it in a way they would never forget. And the man who taught it to them was a thirty-four-year-old American naval officer and a fellow prisoner — Cdr. Richard N. Antrim.

Commander Antrim began the war as the executive officer of the USS *Pope,* a destroyer stationed in the South Pacific, and even before he landed in a Japanese prison camp, he was taking care of his people. In early 1942, Japanese naval aircraft sank Dick Antrim's ship at the Second Battle of the Java Sea. Even though he was wounded, he managed to get 150 crew members off the ship and into the water without losing a man. Then, he prevented them from drifting apart or drowning by tying their life rafts together, and he provided food and water from emergency supplies he had prepared in advance. For three days they floated on the open sea, and his competent leadership kept up their morale. It was a valiant effort,

Richard Antrim was executive officer of the destroyer USS Pope. *When the ship was sunk at the Second Battle of the Java Sea, he helped keep his crew alive.* (Wikimedia Commons Images)

and it saved lives. But on the third day at sea, Commander Antrim and his sailors were captured by a Japanese warship.

They were taken to a deadly Japanese prison camp on the Celebes Islands of Indonesia. The Japanese warrior culture of the era considered any soldier, sailor, or marine who surrendered to be subhuman and deserving of the vilest, most violent mistreatment imaginable. American prisoners of war were routinely starved. They were often beaten and tortured. For the slightest infraction, prisoners were bayoneted or shot to death. Officers who protested the mistreatment of their helpless troops—or even asked questions—were sometimes beheaded. A Japanese prison camp in World War II was a horror hole of starvation, illness, terror, torture, and fear. Violence and death could occur without warning, at any moment.

At Dick Antrim's prison camp, the American POWs also faced the threat of death from friendly fire. From the air, the camp was easily mistaken for a Japanese army post, and the 2,700 POWs there knew that, on any day, they might be killed by an American bomb intended for the enemy. But Dick Antrim was determined to take care of his people. And just as he had done when the Japanese sank his ship, he came up with a plan to protect them from American bombs—at deadly risk to himself. He respectfully asked the prison-camp commandant if his men could dig slit trenches to hide in during air raids. A slit trench offered little protection from a direct hit by a bomb, but it was "busy work" for the prisoners, and the Japanese commandant agreed.

He didn't realize that Dick Antrim's air-raid trenches had another purpose. They were designed to convey a message—a warning that would protect his men and the other American prisoners of war. From the ground, the new American trench system looked anything but suspicious; it appeared to be just a well-engineered series of intersecting trenches. From the air, however, Dick Antrim's prison-camp trench system spelled out a giant *US* – an unmistakable warning to American bombers that the installation below housed American prisoners of war. If the Japanese had discovered his message in the dirt, Dick Antrim surely would have been beheaded. But they didn't. And the plan worked. No bombs fell on Commander Antrim's men or the other POWs.

Again, Dick Antrim had managed to take care of his people.

Then, in the spring of 1942, one of the American POWs—a young naval officer—walked past a Japanese guard and failed to bow low enough. The guard immediately clubbed him to the ground and continued to beat him. Word spread quickly, and soon the camp's entire prisoner population gathered at the site of the beating. The Japanese guard had worked himself into a frenzy, striking the downed American officer again and again. With growing rage, the American POWs watched in helpless frustration. They could do nothing. It was a potentially explosive situation. Nearby, the other Japanese guards fingered the triggers on their rifles, ready to shoot down the first American who tried to stop the savage punishment.

Captured when the Japanese army conquered the Philippines in the spring of 1942, American prisoners of war await their fate under the gaze of armed Japanese guards. (National Archives)

Then Dick Antrim stepped forward.

The prisoner meant no disrespect by the way he bowed, he told the furious guard in a calm voice. Had he not suffered enough? The guard turned from his frenzied blows and looked at Antrim, apparently shocked that a prisoner would dare interfere with his punishment. Before he could direct his fury at Commander Antrim, however, more guards appeared — accompanied by the camp commandant. Antrim made his case to the Japanese officer, interceding for the beaten, bleeding American lying at his feet. The commandant listened to Antrim's plea for mercy and justice — then ordered him to step back. The American prisoner would indeed receive "a just sentence," the officer declared — fifty lashes with a whip.

The commandant departed, and the whipping began: five lashes, six, seven, eight. As the whipping continued, other Japanese guards stepped forward and began kicking the victim. Ten lashes, eleven, twelve — the bloodied American prisoner fell unconscious, and still the beating went on. Thirteen lashes, fourteen, fifteen — the young officer on the ground appeared near death. The assembled POWs were near despair.

Then Dick Antrim again stepped forward.

He knew what could happen if he interfered again: he could be bayoneted or beheaded. But he acted anyway. Stepping forward, he addressed the guards.

He knew what could happen if he interfered again: he could be bayoneted or beheaded. But he acted anyway.

"I'll take the rest!" he said.

The Japanese guards stopped the beating and turned toward Antrim. Calmly, he asked them a question: Would they allow him to take the rest of the prisoner's punishment? "I'll take the rest!" he repeated. His offer stunned the guards. They weren't

accustomed to such self-sacrificing leadership. That wasn't the way of a military dictatorship, or the Japanese warrior code, or anyone they had ever known. Who would offer such a thing? In amazement, they looked at each other. They looked down at the beaten prisoner. They looked back at Dick Antrim.

Then they stopped the beating and walked away.

American prisoners of war secretly observe Independence Day, July 4, 1942, at a Japanese prison camp in the Philippines. If discovered by the Japanese guards, the POWs might have paid for their patriotism with their lives. (National Archives)

The prisoner was saved. The POWs were inspired. And Dick Antrim was later awarded the Congressional Medal of Honor.

Cdr. Richard Antrim made a positive difference in the lives of 2,700 American prisoners of war because he understood a key lesson in leadership: real leaders always take care of their people.

Lesson in Leadership #6

★ ★ ★ ★

Real Leaders Choose to Be Courageous

★ ★ ★ ★

The absence of fear is not the true measure of courage.

Sgt. Mike Fitch.
(Center for Military and Veterans Studies, Coastal Carolina University)

Real courage is doing the right thing despite your fear.

On D-Day, Sgt. Mike Fitch cried all the way to Omaha Beach. Nobody saw him. He didn't want to undermine the morale of the men in his landing craft. And he never tried to duck his duty. But quietly, privately, he cried all the way to Omaha Beach. "I was thinking about my mother," he explained later, "and I figured I'd never see her again." Fitch was a twenty-five-year-old country boy from South Carolina. Like many of his generation, he had experienced a bumpy childhood in the Great Depression, and he adored his mother. She was one of the hardworking, Bible-believing Americans born in the nineteenth century—"the Christian Century," it was called back then, due to the pervasive influence of the Judeo-Christian worldview in American culture. Most members of the Greatest Generation were raised by parents who had grown up in the nineteenth century and who, in turn, instilled those traditional biblical values in their children. Those values, many members of the Greatest Generation would testify, enabled them to weather the Great Depression and win World War II.

Mike Fitch was raised that way: quiet, humble, courteous, helpful. He didn't talk a lot about his personal faith, but he never tried to hide it. And he always tried to live it. It was the compass he trusted to lead him in the right direction. He relied on it early on the morning of June 6, 1944, as his landing craft sped toward the high cliffs of Charlie Sector, the far right flank of Omaha Beach. He did not become fearless — he was still scared — but his faith enabled him to make a critical choice.

Despite his fear, he chose to be courageous.

Despite his fear, he chose to be courageous.

German artillery rounds exploded in the water alongside his landing craft. Other LCTs were hit — blown out of the water, with bodies flying through the air. In his craft, Fitch could hear some men praying. Others were silent. One man kept saying, over and over, "They're gonna get us. They're gonna get us." In the tightly packed landing craft, he only knew two men — the captain and a colonel. Fitch was half of a two-man intelligence and reconnaissance team headed by the captain and went into Omaha Beach attached to the U.S. 29th Infantry Division's 116th Regimental Combat Team. He had met the colonel on training maneuvers back in Ireland — had driven a jeep for him and considered him a friend.

American troops aboard a landing craft head toward Omaha Beach on D-Day, June 6, 1944. (Wikimedia Commons Images)

As the landing craft hit the beach and the front ramp came down, the first men out were Fitch, his captain, and the colonel. Immediately, the colonel was hit by a German mortar round, which exploded and dismembered his body. Sergeant Fitch saw his friend's arm fly by, but he kept going. He and his captain waded through the waist-deep surf and dropped down behind a German iron beach obstacle. "You could hear the bullets ricocheting off that iron obstacle," Fitch later recalled, "and I kept thinking, 'The next one's gonna get me.'" All around them, American soldiers were falling. "The waves were washing the bodies back and forth," Fitch said, "and the water was pink with blood."

When a cloud of smoke rolled over his section of the beach, Fitch and the captain got up and ran for the shelter of a high

A landing craft empties its American troops on Omaha Beach on the morning of D-Day, June 6, 1944. (National Archives)

beachside cliff. Running was hard, Fitch said, because the beach was littered with so many bodies. "You had to jump over the bodies, kind of like hopscotch," he recalled, "and just keep running." As he ran past dead and wounded Americans, one wounded soldier begged Fitch to shoot him and put him out of his pain. "He said, 'Shoot me! Shoot me! Please shoot me!'" Fitch recounted, "but I couldn't do that."

He and his captain made it to the base of the cliff, where they had some protection for a moment—and there they discovered an American paratrooper who had been blown off course after parachuting from his transport plane the night before. One of his arms was broken and he had played dead all night at the foot of the cliff. Lying down beneath the cliff, Fitch looked around him at what would become known as "Bloody Omaha"—and the sight was horrible. Dead and wounded American lay everywhere. Waves were washing up against wrecked landing craft. Destroyed American tanks sat burning and smoking on the beach—and on the bluffs above them they could hear the German artillery, mortar, and machine-gun fire raking the American troops as they waded ashore from their landing craft.

Mike Fitch had never been so afraid in all his life. He wanted to just flatten himself in the sand beneath that cliff, play dead, and do nothing. But he knew that would be wrong. He *had* to do something. So he suppressed his fear and chose to be courageous. He and his captain and the injured paratrooper could see deadly enemy fire coming from a concrete German artillery and machine-gun installation above them—a fortification that American troops commonly called a "pillbox." It was actually a cleverly camouflaged German defense work officially known as WN-73, and it was killing

American soldiers by the droves. Fitch and the two others decided to attack the installation. They crawled up the side of the cliff until they were a few yards beneath it and tossed hand grenades at it. The grenades exploded and did nothing. They tried again. Still nothing—but suddenly *German* hand grenades began falling on them from the top of the cliff. They managed to get out of the way and opened fire on the German pillbox with their rifles—causing another rain of German hand grenades from the cliff. Again they escaped harm, but the enemy pillbox was still firing. So they concocted a plan: the captain, who had been a college ballplayer, would pick up the German hand grenades and throw them out on the beach to explode, while Fitch and the paratrooper would keeping firing at the pillbox. They put the plan in action, firing at the pillbox and causing more German hand grenades to drop on them—which the captain caught and tossed away. But the enemy installation was still firing, still killing American soldiers on the beach.

Then Fitch had an idea. He and the paratrooper fired their rifles into the opening on the front of the German pillbox—the gun port—aiming toward the ceiling and trying to ricochet their bullets around the inside of the pillbox where the enemy troops were operating the installation's guns. The hand grenades kept falling, and the captain kept fielding them, but the gunfire from the German pillbox suddenly stopped. The enemy crew was either down or driven away. They had done it. They had stopped the murderous fire from WN-73—it was silenced forever.

Sgt. Mike Fitch survived Bloody Omaha and spent the rest of the war serving in advance of American lines as a reconnaissance scout and army sniper. He was engaged in combat almost daily, and much of it was hand to hand. "You could never relax," he said.

"You were always thinking about what might happen to you next. You *had* to think that way. That's the only way you could survive." He would earn two Purple Hearts, two Bronze Stars, the Sharpshooter Medal, and the French Croix de Guerre.

And he was always afraid.

But until the war ended, he never stopped fighting. How did he do it? The answer: Sgt. Mike Fitch—a common soldier of uncommon valor—

Within hours of the capture of Omaha Beach, American troops and equipment headed off the beach and inland. By the end of the day on June 6, more than 150,000 Allied troops were ashore in Normandy. (Library of Congress)

practiced an indispensable lesson in leadership. Real leaders choose to be courageous.

Lesson in Leadership #7

★ ★ ★ ★

Real Leaders Are Always Willing to Do What They Ask of Others

★ ★ ★ ★

Mitchell Paige joined the U.S. Marines two weeks after his eighteenth birthday.

Sgt. Mitchell Paige. (U.S. Marine Corps Archive)

And he walked more than two hundred miles to do it.

A few weeks after he graduated from high school in 1936, he left his home in McKeesport, Pennsylvania and hiked to a Marine Corps recruiting station in Baltimore, Maryland. He caught a couple of rides, but for most of the long journey, he walked—for more than two hundred miles. Along the way, he ate sandwiches and apples from a sack his mother had packed for the trip. In it, he discovered a note she had written. "Trust in the Lord, son," it read, "and he will guide you always."

Mitch Paige took his mother's advice to heart and tried to follow it even amid the rough-and-tumble life of an American marine in wartime. Eventually, he found himself in the South Pacific in one of the bloodiest engagements of World War II: the battle for Guadalcanal. By then he was a sergeant in the First Marine Division and commanded a machine-gun platoon. His men looked to him for leadership—and he gave it to them even before they entered battle.

His platoon was equipped with four obsolete .30-caliber machine guns left over from World War I. The guns tended to shoot high and also had a slow rate of fire. The aging weapons, he feared, would get his men killed in battle. He could have left the problem to someone else, but that was not his way: Mitchell Paige would not pass the buck. He never asked his men to do what he was unwilling to do himself. So he pondered the problem awhile, then had the platoon's machine guns brought to his tent. There, he drilled holes in the weapons' bolts and installed newer,

U.S. Marines take a break on Guadalcanal in 1942. Guadalcanal was the first major Allied offensive in the Pacific, and victory would require six months of fighting, with more than seven thousand American casualties. (National Archives)

stronger trigger springs. His modifications made the guns much more accurate and almost tripled their rate of fire. Thanks to Paige's leadership, his platoon landed on Guadalcanal with highly accurate, rapid-firing weapons.

They would need them.

On October 25, 1942, Sergeant Paige and his four-gun platoon were sent to the front and deployed in the dark of night to help defend a critically important airstrip called Henderson Field. At any moment, Japanese troops were expected to launch a powerful attack to reclaim the airfield. Paige's platoon was deployed on a forward battle line between two marine rifle companies—first in line for any assault. "You have to hold this line," Paige's company commander told him. The First Marine Division was moving forward to deploy in force, but until they were fully up and in place, Sergeant Paige and the thin line of troops at the front had to hold back the enemy.

A patrol of U.S. Marines wades through a river on Guadalcanal. (National Archives)

What if the Japanese attacked in the night? Paige knew that the enemy sometimes came charging out of the darkness in surprise Banzai attacks. How could he protect his men and their mission from a surprise assault? Then an idea came to him—but it required risky action. Somebody would have to crawl forward in the darkness in advance of the front line. He could have called for volunteers or ordered some of his men forward, but again he took the lead. He ordered his men to collect their empty C-ration cans—the tin cans in which rations were issued—and put an empty cartridge casing in each can. Then he crawled forward in advance of their position and strung the tin cans on a trip wire, setting up a makeshift alarm system to warn of a surprise assault.

That night the Japanese attacked. As they advanced through the darkness, they stumbled into the line of cans, breaking the night silence with a loud racket—and Paige's platoon promptly unleashed a deadly fire. Just as Paige had hoped, the platoon's modified, rapid-fire machine guns evened the odds and stopped the enemy charge. But the Japanese attacked again. This time they stormed over their dead and wounded and broke through the marines' defensive line. The fighting was up close, hand to hand, and horrible. Again, the Japanese were driven back—but Paige's thirty-three-man platoon had been whittled down to half-strength, and the rifle companies on both sides had withdrawn.

They were hopelessly outnumbered. Why not quit and retreat? Why not take the wounded and fall back? Why not let the marines to the rear battle the next Banzai charges? But if they retreated, Paige knew, other marines would have to take their places and do the fighting. He would not do it. And neither would his marines. Instead, they chose to remain in the front and face the enemy. "We just fought them hand to hand all night long," Paige would later recount. After repeated attacks, Paige realized he was the only man in his platoon still able to stand. Everyone else was dead or too wounded to fight. Soon, the Japanese charged again, running right over his foxhole in the darkness. He turned his machine gun around and fired into the rear of the attacking enemy troops — until the gun jammed. Then he raced from one machine gun to the next, pouring fire into the enemy ranks from the rear. It broke the Japanese charge — and the survivors disappeared back into the darkness from where they had come.

Finally, as dawn was breaking on Guadalcanal, reinforcements

Battle-tested marines in the Pacific man a .30-caliber machine gun and await another Japanese attack. Sergeant Paige modified his platoon's machine guns to increase accuracy and rate of fire. (U.S. Navy Historical Foundation)

reached his position, just as the Japanese mounted another attack. Paige cradled one of his machine guns in his arms, shouted for the fresh troops to follow

Instead, they chose to remain in the front and face the enemy.

him — and charged the advancing enemy line. The counterattack was too much for the Japanese and they retreated. Finally, the fighting ended. Paige plopped down in a foxhole. He too was wounded — and exhausted. Searching for something to stop a bleeding bayonet wound, he emptied his field pack. Out fell his pocket-size New Testament, and to his amazement it was open to Proverbs chapter three — the Scripture his mother had packed in his lunch sack so long ago: "Trust in the Lord with all your heart, and lean not on your own understanding; in all your ways acknowledge Him, and He will direct your paths."

The path Mitchell Paige chose on Guadalcanal that long and deadly night was the way of a leader. It saved lives, earned Paige the Congressional Medal of Honor, and demonstrated a central truth of leadership: real leaders are always willing to do what they ask of others.

Lesson in Leadership #8

Real Leaders Demonstrate Integrity

★ ★ ★ ★

Twenty-two-year-old Desmond Doss was willing to go to war.

Army Medic Desmond Doss. (U.S. Army Medical Department)

He just didn't want to take a weapon.

Doss was a devout Christian, and while most Christians believed they had a biblical right to self-defense in a just war—especially fighting the evils of Nazi Germany and Imperial Japan—Desmond Doss did not. His conscience prohibited him from taking a human life. In the spring of 1942, he was drafted into the U.S. Army and was designated a "conscientious objector."

It was a title Doss did not like. He did not object to serving his country in uniform, he said; he just didn't want to kill anybody. Therefore, he considered himself to be a "conscientious *cooperator*." He was a mountain boy—a "hillbilly" from the Blue Ridge Mountains of Virginia. When he got his draft notice, he was working in a shipyard, which qualified him for a draft exemption.

He didn't take it.

Instead, he went into the army as a conscientious objector and asked to serve as a combat medic. "I felt like it was an honor to serve God and my country according to the dictates of my conscience," he said later. Many of his fellow soldiers didn't see it that way. They considered conscientious objectors to be draft dodgers, and they constantly harassed and ridiculed Doss—until they reached the combat zone in the South Pacific. There, the tormenting stopped. Why? Because Desmond Doss—a medic in the U.S. Army's Seventy-Seventh Infantry Division—risked his life again and again to rescue wounded soldiers. When Doss's infantry was first exposed to combat, some of his main tormentors turned and ran. As they ran back, Doss ran forward. His bravery became legendary. When fighting began, it was said, Desmond Doss would grab his medic's kit and head for the sound of the guns.

In late April of 1945, the Seventy-Seventh Infantry Division was engaged in the bloody fighting to capture Okinawa. They were ordered to drive the Japanese from a high plateau called Hacksaw Ridge. Other American troops had tried and failed to capture the sprawling plateau, which was heavily fortified and honeycombed with caves filled with Japanese troops. The Seventy-Seventh boldly climbed a forty-foot-high cliff, then assaulted the Japanese positions. Eventually, Hacksaw Ridge would be captured, but the Seventy-Seventh Division's first attack was a deadly failure. Japanese artillery, mortar, and machine-gun fire turned the plateau into a slaughter pen. It was littered with American dead. And countless wounded Americans were left lying on the plateau under Japanese fire.

Someone had to rescue them. But there was only one medic available: Desmond Doss. Above him was the plateau — Hacksaw Ridge. To get there, he had to climb the forty-foot-high cliff. Then he had to somehow get the wounded back down to safety. As he stood looking up at the cliff, some of his buddies offered him a weapon. He shook his head no. "I'll leave the fighting to y'all," he said. "I'll just do the patching up." Then up he went and over the high cliff to the plateau — which he found carpeted with American wounded. How could one man help so many? And how could he even get them back down the cliff?

That's where Desmond Doss's personal integrity showed itself in a mighty way. Forgetting about himself, he concentrated solely on saving his fellow soldiers. Why? What motivated him to risk his life in what was obviously an impossible, hopeless task?

"Love."

An estimated 110,000 Japanese troops defended Okinawa. They were experienced, well equipped, and determined — and most refused to surrender. (Wikimedia Commons Images)

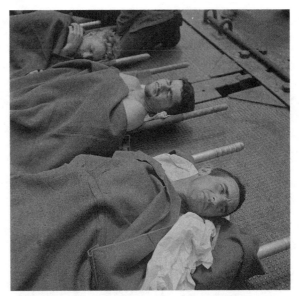

Wounded American troops wait to be taken below on an American warship anchored off Okinawa. Naval corpsmen and army medics provided emergency treatment in the front until American wounded could be moved to army or navy hospitals in the rear or offshore. (National Archives)

That's how he later explained it. It was love, he said, that motivated him to risk all in one of World War II's bloodiest battles. "I loved my men, and they loved me," he explained. "I just couldn't give them up." First, he figured out how to get the wounded off the cliff. "God brought to my mind how to get them off," he later said. He rigged up a harness hooked to a scraggly tree on the side of the cliff and used that to lower the wounded to safety. But he could only lower one man at a time.

And so that's what he did. He focused on saving one man—just one. Then he would focus on another, and another, and another. "I just kept praying, 'Lord, help me get one more,'" he later recounted. "I just kept praying that until I got every man off."

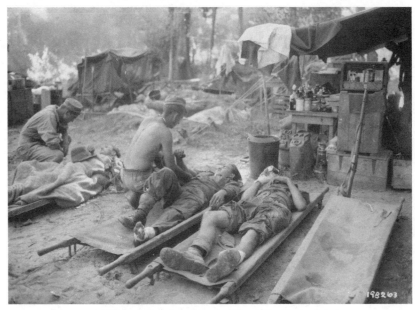

Army medics treat Allied wounded at a jungle aid station. When fighting occurred, it was said, Medic Desmond Doss would grab his medical kit and head for the sound of the guns. (National Archives)

And he did. In a miraculous feat, Desmond Doss treated and dragged one wounded soldier after another across the plateau, then lowered them down the cliff to safety on his rigged-up harness, one at a time. He rescued every wounded soldier on Hacksaw Ridge. And despite the Japanese fire, none was hit again. Nor was Doss. Afterward, army investigators were sent to examine the extraordinary rescue, and they concluded that Desmond Doss, the "conscientious cooperator," had saved seventy-five wounded American soldiers from Hacksaw Ridge. Some said it was really more than a hundred.

And the soldiers who had once ridiculed Desmond Doss for his faith? Never again would that happen. The soldiers who served with Doss showed how they felt about him when he was later wounded on Okinawa. He was hit by shrapnel from a Japanese hand grenade, then was wounded again when he insisted on rolling off his stretcher so another solider could be taken to safety. Word came back from the field hospital that Desmond Doss would recover from his wounds—but he had lost his pocket Bible somewhere on the battlefield. An entire battalion of troops dropped everything and picked over the battlefield until they found Doss's Bible, which they sent to him. It was an act of selflessness and integrity by the soldiers Doss loved—and it had been modeled for them by the man they had once ridiculed.

No one mocked Desmond Doss for his faith and his integrity ever again. He became the only conscientious objector—and "conscientious cooperator"—of World War II to receive the Congressional Medal of Honor. When saluted as a hero, the legendary rescuer of Hacksaw Ridge, he demonstrated his humility and integrity again. "I'm not a hero," he said. "I want the glory to go to God."

Desmond Doss typified lesson in leadership #8: real leaders demonstrate integrity.

It was an act of selflessness and integrity—modeled by the man they had once ridiculed.

Lesson in Leadership #9

Real Leaders Always Arrange for a Successor

Lt. Charles L. Thomas was "a bloody mess."

Lt. Charles L. Thomas.
(U.S. Army Military
History Center)

But he refused to leave his men leaderless.

It was December of 1944, and Lt. Charles Thomas was a company commander in an army tank destroyer battalion—at age twenty-four. He wasn't a professional soldier. He was an assembly-line worker at an auto plant in Detroit and a college student. At least that's what he was doing when the war came. But then he joined the army, wound up in Officers Candidate School, graduated with a second lieutenant's commission, and eventually found himself commanding Company C of the 614th Tank Destroyer Battalion on the border of France and Germany. He was young for a company commander—and he was also one of the few black officers commanding combat troops in the U.S. Army.

The U.S. Armed Forces were still officially segregated, and the

614th Tank Destroyer Battalion was an all-black outfit. It wasn't famous like the "Tuskegee Airmen" of the Army Air Force or the "Black Panthers" of the 761st Tank Battalion, but it too was composed entirely of black troops. In December of 1944, it was engaged in battle, and Lieutenant Thomas and Company C were on the front lines. A month earlier, the 614th had joined Gen. George Patton's Third Army. As Patton led his forces toward the German border, he had radioed back to the rear for reinforcements — and he wanted the best armored unit available. He was informed that the best unit on hand was an all-black outfit — the 614th. In unmistakable terms, Patton radioed back that he didn't care what color they were. He wanted the best.

And so, the 614th Tank Destroyer Battalion — including Lieutenant Thomas and Company C — gained their baptism of fire in Patton's Third Army. They met Patton's expectations, advancing at one point through what was described as "a hail of fire." In early December, the battalion was transferred to the Seventh Army as part of a special task force organized to drive German forces from a stronghold at the French town of Climbach, located near the German border.

The town was perched on a rise surrounded by high, forested ridges and overlooked an open valley. It was defended by a large force of German infantry, which was supported by German artillery and a contingent of German Panzer tanks. The planned American attack called for Lieutenant Thomas and a platoon from his company to open fire on the German positions from the valley floor with four artillery pieces. Meanwhile, an infantry force composed of 250 troops would circle around and surprise the Germans with a flank attack.

Troops from the all-black 614th Tank Destroyer Battalion man a three-inch gun.
(National Archives)

Lieutenant Thomas's four artillery pieces were towed by army M2 half-tracks—and Thomas was in the lead vehicle, following the task-force commander on a narrow road through the woods toward Climbach. On the edge of the valley outside town, the commander stopped his command car and called the task force to a halt. Ahead lay the valley and its open terrain—all within easy range of the German artillery and tanks. It was an obvious killing field. The little column of half-tracks and trucks waited there for a long moment, with their engines idling. Then Lieutenant Thomas ordered his half-track forward, pulled up beside the command car, and volunteered to lead the way. The task-force commander hesitated a moment, then agreed.

Off Thomas went in the lead, followed by his platoon of half-tracks, artillery pieces, and ammo trucks. The Germans held their fire until the little column was well into the valley—then they opened up with tanks, artillery, and machineguns. The first volley blew out the tires on Thomas' half-track and shattered its windshield, seriously wounding the young lieutenant with glass shards. Thomas did not stay put, however. His half-track carried a crew of two and seven soldiers in the rear. To cover his men as they escaped from the disabled vehicle, Thomas climbed on top, manned the half-track's .50-caliber machine gun, and opened up on the enemy.

Then he jumped down from the half-track to deploy his artillery—and was immediately hit by a burst of machine-gun fire. He was seriously wounded. One soldier said it was as if the

U.S. armored troops in half-tracks tow their artillery pieces into position during prewar army maneuvers. In December of 1944, Lieutenant Thomas and his battery from the 614th Tank Destroyer Battalion used such aging weapons with powerful effect against German troops at Climbach, France. (U.S. Army Military History Center)

lieutenant had been "cross-stitched" by bullets. Thomas was "a bloody mess," remarked another soldier. Somebody called for medics to rush Thomas to the rear, but he waved them off. Despite his wounds, he insisted on staying with his troops, deploying his artillery and opening a punishing fire on the German positions. He looked as though he might bleed to death in minutes, and his men urged him to go to the rear—but he refused. He would not leave them leaderless. There were other officers nearby who could take over, but they were inexperienced and Thomas would not hear of it. He sent word to the rear that he was not leaving his men until an officer of equal experience was sent forward to replace him. He would *not* put his men in the hands of a greenhorn.

Thomas's four artillery pieces were no match for the enemy's Panzer tanks or their heavier artillery, but he had trained his platoon well, and they directed such a precise, searing fire on the enemy positions that the Germans frantically turned every gun they had on them. One by one, the American guns were knocked out and more than half of Thomas's platoon was wounded. Meanwhile, it seemed clear to everyone that Lieutenant Thomas would soon bleed to death if his wounds were not treated. But he would not leave his men, not until a competent successor came forward to relieve him. His troops were fighting hard—he could see that and he was proud of them—but he wanted to inspire them to *keep* fighting and not give up. "Seeing me hurt and still doing my job," he later said, "pushed them to even greater effort."

Finally, an experienced combat veteran came forward. Thomas was satisfied—his men would be in good hands. And so he finally allowed himself to be carried to the rear. He was so shot up—so badly wounded—that his troops figured they would never see him again. But even in his absence, he still served them, because his leadership example **Thomas was** had inspired them, and the successor he **satisfied—his men** demanded was a capable **would be in good** leader. Like Thomas, his **hands.** troops did not give up. Even when three of their four guns were disabled, they kept pouring deadly fire into the enemy positions with their remaining artillery piece. When one artilleryman was shot down, another would rush forward to take his place.

And the lone gun kept pounding the enemy.

Eventually, it ran low on ammunition. Only a few artillery shells remained. Then one of Thomas's soldiers got behind the wheel of an ammo truck and headed to the front. An officer tried to stop him, shouting that it was a suicide mission, but the soldier would not be stopped—and under heavy fire he drove fresh ammunition right up to the gun and kept it firing. For more than four hours, these black American soldiers, whose courage and competence had once been questioned by some, kept a sustained artillery fire raining on the enemy positions. Desperate to stop what appeared to be a full battalion of artillery, the Germans finally launched an infantry assault against Thomas's troops—which were by then reduced to half-strength. But the surviving artillerymen grabbed their rifles and opened such a fierce defensive fire against the enemy attack that the Germans fell back in retreat.

And then the enemy fire abruptly stopped. Everything became quiet. Moments later someone brought the news: the Germans in Climbach had been defeated. Their tanks and artillery had been destroyed, captured, or driven away. The enemy troops had become so desperately focused on stopping the artillery fire coming from Thomas's depleted battery that they had failed to guard their flanks—and the American infantry had managed to successfully launch their surprise flank attack. The enemy was defeated. The town was captured. And U.S. forces were now poised to enter Nazi Germany.

Throughout the American lines, the story began to spread about Lieutenant Thomas and the platoon of soldiers from the all-black 614th Tank Destroyer Battalion—the American

American infantry examine a battered but still formidable fortification captured from German forces at Climbach. Was some of the damage inflicted by Lieutenant Thomas's hard-fighting artillerymen? (National Archives)

artillerymen who would not give up. The white officer who commanded the task force stated that the actions of Lieutenant Thomas and his platoon were "the most magnificent display of mass heroism I have ever witnessed." Eventually, Thomas's tiny band of soldiers was awarded more than a dozen bronze stars, three Silver Stars, two Distinguished Service Medals, and one Congressional Medal of Honor—which went to Lt. Charles L. Thomas. He was a man who had kept his troops fighting even in his absence, who understood that real leaders always arrange for a successor.

Lesson in Leadership #10

Real Leaders Lead by Example

★ ★ ★ ★

The young lieutenant looked nothing like John Wayne.

Maj. Richard Winters. (World War II Foundation)

But he became a genuine hero.

He was a soft-spoken twenty-two-year-old from rural Pennsylvania, quiet, humble, devout, not a boaster or a bossy type. He had volunteered for the army because he wanted to do his duty, get the war over as quickly as possible, and get back home. He had the makings of a true leader, and his superiors saw it immediately. He was selected for Officers Candidate School and did well there in his quiet, wise, and responsible way. And there he decided he wanted to be an Airborne officer. Others noticed that the troops under him always seemed motivated to try harder and do better. And soon he was promoted from lieutenant to captain. Later, others would analyze his leadership skills. What was it about this quiet, humble young officer that so inspired the troops he led?

He had a vision—he understood the mission and was committed to it. And his men were better for it. He was a self-starter. And so his men willingly followed him. He was willing to take responsibility when things went wrong. And everyone respected him for it. He persevered under hardship. And so his men did too. He took care of his people. And his people loved him for it. He chose to be courageous. And those around him were inspired to do the same. He was willing to do what he asked of others. And so others willingly obeyed him. He demonstrated integrity. So his men trusted and respected him. He arranged for successors to follow him. And his troops were not left leaderless.

And he led by example.

When other officers were off in town on a weekend pass, he was often found leading new recruits on a field march. Why? Because he believed it was his duty to do it if *they* had to. He knew that the most effective leadership—*real* leadership—came from personal example. He didn't shirk the hard duty, the dirty work, the jobs nobody wanted. *And he didn't complain.* Why not? Because he wanted to lead by example. And he did: he set an example of genuine character, personal faith, and duty done well.

He rose from captain to major.

He was the officer under whom soldiers *wanted* to serve—the man they *wanted* to follow. He led them into Normandy on D-Day, parachuting into enemy territory with the 101st Airborne. When he drew a deadly assignment—to knock out a German artillery battery firing on Utah Beach—his soldiers followed him without question. And his leadership by example paid off. He and his men were ordered to attack a battery of German artillery on a farm in Normandy called Brecourt Manor: thirteen Americans against artillery manned **He was the man** by fifty troops. In a classic flank assault, they took out **they *wanted* to** one German artillery piece **follow.** after another until the entire

battery was silenced. And they did it with such teamwork and such efficiency — and with so few casualties — that, for more than half a century, West Point cadets would be taught the tactics used at what would become known as the "Assault at Brecourt Manor."

He was eventually promoted to battalion commander — still leading by example but now leading larger numbers of American troops. He had risen from lieutenant to captain to major. He led

Their heads shaved in the style of Mohawk Indians, paratroopers from the 101st Airborne apply war paint while waiting alongside their aircraft. Some of the "Screaming Eagles" made the drop on D-Day bedecked in such style. (U.S. Army Signal Corps)

On D-Day, American C-47 troop transports and gliders circle above the hedgerow fields of Normandy near the village of Ste. Mère Eglise. U.S. paratroopers landed by parachute and gliders on D-Day. (Library of Congress)

In the skies above France, an American paratrooper prepares to jump from his Dakota troop transport on D-Day. Airborne troops went in early on D-Day to seize and hold key causeways, crossroads, and bridges for the main invasion force landing on the beaches. (National Archives)

American toops through Operation Market Garden in Holland, through the battle of the Bulge in Belgium, across the Rhine River into Germany, and until the end of the war in Europe. He proved himself to be a leader who led by example. Outside of his regiment, however, no one knew about his extraordinary model of leadership. But the men who had followed him into harm's way knew about it.

And they never forgot it.

In the decades to follow, those aging paratroopers—veterans of the 101st Airborne's 506th Parachute Infantry Regiment—would remember him and his leadership of "Easy" Company. And that "Band of Brothers," as they would become known, would always love him and respect him because of his personal example of leadership. Long after the war ended, when a famous historian would come to interview them about their heroic and bloody odyssey through World War II, all of them would mention the man who led by example: Maj. Richard Winters—Dick Winters.

The story of Easy Company and Dick Winters' leadership would become a bestselling book: *Band of Brothers,* by Stephen Ambrose. And the world would learn of Dick Winters, who would come to represent the best of the Greatest Generation. He was a man of character, faith, and duty; a leader who understood the ultimate lesson in leadership: real leaders lead by example.

Lessons in Leadership from the Greatest Generation

Real leaders have a vision.

Real leaders are self-starters.

Real leaders always take responsibility.

Real leaders persevere.

Real leaders always take care of their people.

Real leaders choose to be courageous.

Real leaders are always willing to do what they ask of others.

Real leaders demonstrate integrity.

Real leaders always arrange for a successor.

Real leaders lead by example.

Selected Bibliography

★ ★ ★ ★

Alexander, Joseph H. *The Battle History of the U.S. Marines: A Fellowship of Valor.* New York: HarperCollins, 1997.

Alexander, Larry. *Biggest Brother: The Life of Major Richard Winters.* New York: New American Library, 2005.

Ambrose, Steven E. *Band of Brothers: E Company, 506th Regiment, 101st Airborne from Normandy to Hitler's Eagle's Nest.* New York: Simon and Schuster, 2002.

____. *The Supreme Commander: The War Years of General Dwight D. Eisenhower.* Garden City, NY: Doubleday, 1970.

Anderson, Richard C. *Cracking Hitler's Atlantic Wall.* Mechanicsburg, PA: Stackpole Books, 2010.

____. *Peace Was in Their Hearts: Conscientious Objectors in World War II.* Los Gatos, CA: Correlan, 1994.

Appleman, Roy Edgar, James M. Burns, Russell A. Gugeler, and John Stevens. *Okinawa: The Last Battle.* Washington, D.C.: U.S. Government Printing Office, 1948.

Arnold, James, and Starr Sinton. *U.S. Commanders of World War II: Navy and USMC.* Oxford: Osprey, 2002.

Bando, Mark. *Vanguard of the Crusade: The 101st Airborne Division in World War II.* Havertown, PA: Casemate, 2012.

Berstein, Adam. "Col. Mitchell Paige, Medal of Honor Recipient, Dies." *Washington Post,* November 18, 2003.

"Burial Set April 3 in National Cemetery for Medal of Honor Winner Desmond Doss." *Chattanoogan,* March 23, 2006.

Butcher, Harry C. *My Three Years with Eisenhower: The Personal Diary of Captain Harry C. Butcher.* New York: Simon and Schuster, 1948.

Connolly, Cindy. "North Platte Canteen Dished Up Instant Hospitality, Friendship." *Omaha World-Herald,* June 1, 1994.

Doss, Desmond Thomas. Oral History. Veterans History Project, Library of Congress.

Eisenhower, Dwight D. *Crusade in Europe: A Personal Account of World War II.* New York: Doubleday, 1948.

Fitch, Mike. Oral History Interview. Center for Military and Veterans Studies, Coastal Carolina University, 2011.

Frank, Richard B. *Guadalcanal: The Definitive Account of the Landmark Battle.* New York: Penguin Group, 1992.

Friedman, Kenneth I. *Morning of the Rising Sun: The Heroic Story of the Battle of Guadalcanal.* New York: BookSurge, 2007.

Gragg, Rod, Dennis Reed, and David Parker. "Back to the Battlefield: A D-Day Veteran Returns to Omaha Beach." Conway. SC: Southern Communications, 2008.

Greene, Bob. *Once Upon a Small Town: The Miracle of the North Platte Canteen.* New York: HarperCollins, 2002.

Hallas, James. *Killing Ground on Okinawa: The Battle for Sugar Loaf Hill.* Annapolis: Naval Institute Press, 2007.

Hargis, Roger, and Starr Sinton. *World War II Medal of Honor Recipients: Navy and USMC.* Oxford: Osprey, 2003.

Harris, Brayton. *Admiral Nimitz: The Commander of the Pacific Ocean Theater.* New York: Palgrave Macmillan, 2011.

Harris, Mark Jonathan, with Franklin D. Mitchell and Steven J. Schecter. *The Homefront: America During World War II.* New York: Perigee Books, 1994.

Herndon, Booten. *The Unlikeliest Hero: Desmond Doss, Conscientious Objector.* Nampa, ID: Pacific Press, 1967.

Hoyt, Edwin Palmer. *How They Won the War in the Pacific: Nimitz and His Admirals.* Guilford, CT: Globe Pequot, 2000.

Kimbel, L. F. *United Service Organization: Five Years of Service.* Washington, D.C.: United Service Organization, 1946.

Knox, Chuck. *The Muted Trumpet's Call.* Bloomington, IN: AuthorHouse, 2011.

Lankford, Jim. "Gamecocks at War: The 614th Tank Destroyer Battalion." *On Point: The Online Journal of Army History,* February 9, 2012.

Lee, Ulysses. *The Employment of Negro Troops.* Washington, D.C.: U.S. Government Printing Office, 1963.

Motley, Mary P. *The Invisible Soldier: The Experience of the Black Soldier, World War II.* Detroit: Wayne State University Press, 1975.

Moore, Bob, and Kent Fedorowich, *Prisoners of War and Their Captors in World War II.* Oxford: Berg, 1996.

Moore, Christopher Paul. *Fighting for America: Black Soldiers – The Unsung Heroes of World War II.* New York: Ballantine Books, 2006.

Myers, Max, ed. *Ours to Hold It High: A History of the 77th Infantry Division in World War II by the Men Who Were There.* Washington, D.C.: Infantry Journal Press, 1947.

"On the Home Front: North Platte Canteen," http://www.nebraskastudies.org.

Owens, Ron. *Medal of Honor: Facts and Figures.* Paduca: Turner Publishing, 2004.

Paige, Mitchell. *A Marine Named Mitch: An Autobiography of Mitchell Paige, Colonel, U.S. Marine Corps.* New York: Vantage, 1975.

Potter, Elmer B. *Nimitz.* Annapolis: Naval Institute Press, 1976.

Prados, John. *Normandy Crucible: The Decisive Battle that Shaped World War II in Europe.* New York: New American Library, 2011.

Richardson, Glenda. *Medal of Honor Recipients.* Hauppauge, NY: Novinka Books, 2003.

Ryan, Cornelius. *The Longest Day: June 6, 1944.* New York: Simon and Schuster, 1959.

Symonds, Craig L. *The Naval Institute Historical Atlas of the U.S. Navy.* Annapolis: Naval Institute Press, 2001.

Wilson, Joe. *The 761st "Black Panther" Tank Battalion.* Jefferson, NC: McFarland, 1999.

Winchel, Meghan H. *Good Girls, Good Food, Good Fun: The Story of USO Hostesses in World War II.* Chapel Hill: University of North Carolina Press, 2008.

Winters, Dick, and Cole C. Kingseed. *Beyond Band of Brothers: The War Memoirs of Major Dick Winters.* New York: Penguin Group, 2008.

Zaloga, Steven. *D-Day 1944: Omaha Beach.* Oxford: Osprey, 2012.